# THIS BOOK BELONGS TO:

_____

_____

# Free Bonus Gift Giveaway!!

## Sign up on explorearthursworld.com to receive your gift!

ISBN: 978-1-950904-04-4 (Paperback)
ISBN: 978-1-950904-03-7 (Hardcover)
Library of Congress Control Number: TXu002149987
Edited by Jennifer Rees
Cover design and Illustrations by Judith San Nicolás (JudithSDesign&Creativity)

# USA

## DESTINATIONS THAT
## SPARK OUR FASCINATIONS

### GENE LIPEN

| Departures ✈ | | | 10:23 |
|---|---|---|---|
| Flight No. | Deaprting To | Time | Status |
| US 055 | Salt Lake City | 13:35 | On Time |
| UA 6775 | New York | 13:38 | On Time |
| UA 7786 | Chicago ORD | 13:51 | On Time |
| AC 664 | San Francisco | 14:41 | On Time |
| WS 1233 | Phoenix | 15:05 | On Time |
| AA 632 | Oakland | 15:15 | On Time |
| QX 2771 | Seattle | 15:37 | On Time |
| UA 7764 | Denver | 16:17 | On Time |
| AC 8820 | Miami | 16:40 | On Time |
| UA 6533 | San Francisco | 16:53 | On Time |
| WS 1424 | Las Vegas | 17:13 | On Time |

He packed up his luggage, amazement in sight,
Arthur's adventure is about to take flight.

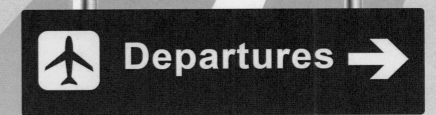

Let's wish him the best on his journey and state:
"Excitement is building,
We just cannot wait!"

Carved on the side of a towering rock,
You will find this colossal and well-known landmark.
Four famous presidents, larger than life,
Iconic and confident, they look almost alive,

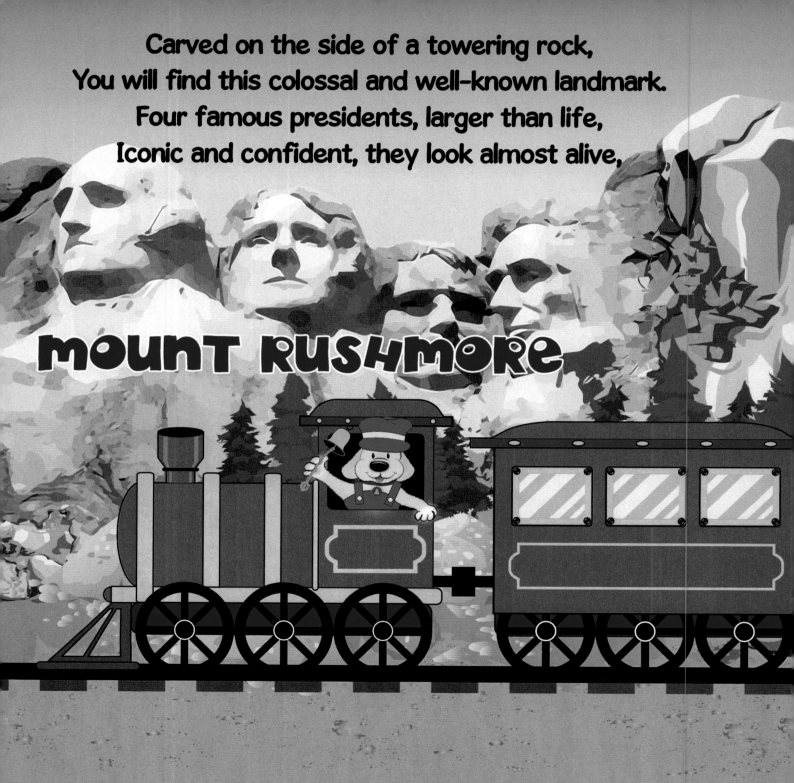

MOUNT RUSHMORE

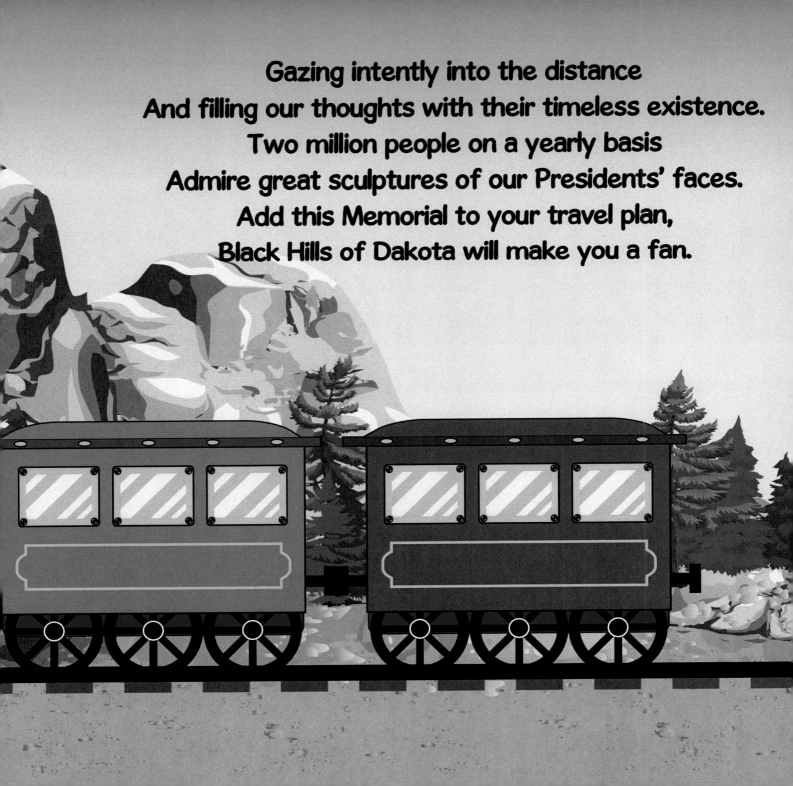

Gazing intently into the distance
And filling our thoughts with their timeless existence.
Two million people on a yearly basis
Admire great sculptures of our Presidents' faces.
Add this Memorial to your travel plan,
Black Hills of Dakota will make you a fan.

# YELLOWSTONE

Sitting above a gigantic hot spot,
With red molten rock rising straight to the top,
We find a preserve full of natural wonders
Covered in mountains, lakes, rivers, and canyons.

From bears to bison, elk and deer, to wolves,
There is so much to see and no time to snooze—
Half the world's geysers call it their home,
The one named Old Faithful is very well known.
This National Park was the first of its kind
To protect rugged beauty and wildlife combined.
Grab your comfy shoes, make the trip, and you'll see
How wonderful and graceful our planet can be.

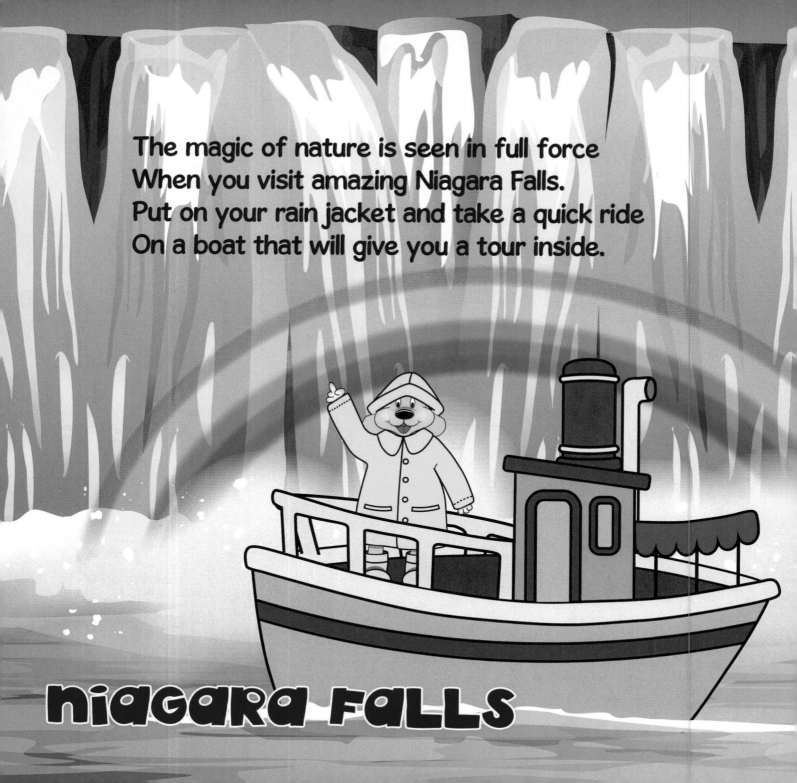

The magic of nature is seen in full force
When you visit amazing Niagara Falls.
Put on your rain jacket and take a quick ride
On a boat that will give you a tour inside.

NIAGARA FALLS

You will learn how our water is used as a source
Of electrical power for four million homes.
Countless visitors yearly flock
To the magic of Falls in the state of New York.
Set your sights on this wonder and you will agree
How powerful nature can really be.

Well known for its cable suspension design
On the beautiful cliffs of Pacific coastline,
Stands the Golden Gate Bridge, strait of one mile wide,
Graceful, majestic, California's pride.

# GOLDEN GATE

Put together with one million rivets of steel,
Makes this famous bridge so unique, what a thrill.
Take a ride, grab your bike, or enjoy a long walk
On a bridge that is perfect for pics in thick fog.
Pause for a moment, reflect, and you'll see
Why this bridge makes us feel so amazing and free.

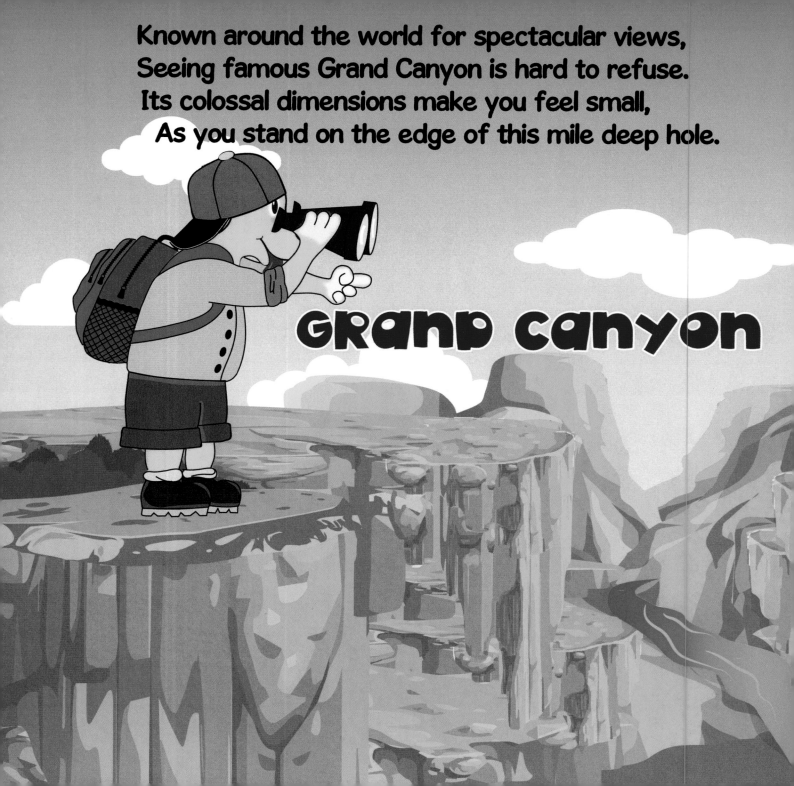

The temperature range varies vastly throughout,
From frost in some parts and others in drought.
A powerful river carved this sight in the process,
While exposing strange plants and historical fossils.
Its intricate landscape and vistas amaze,
You won't take your eyes off these tremendous displays.

# MANHATTAN

Known to the locals as simply "the City,"
With miles of skyscrapers, it stands looking pretty.
Times Square experience is a tourist must,
With countless lights, tons of people and shops.
To escape from the hustle and bustle galore,
Central Park is the place to relax and see more.

From concerts, fun tours, and a colorful zoo,
Time will simply fly by—you won't know what to do.
Seeing all of the shows and museums is tough,
One trip to Manhattan is just not enough.

Tucked away in the hills of Sierra Nevada,
Sits this National Park, nature lovers nirvana.
Amazing adventure awaits you inside
This is animal turf, keep your eyes open wide.

YOSEMITE

From huge waterfalls that perplex and surprise,
To Sequoia old trees, gigantic in size.
You will find yourself hiking from morning till night,
Exploring the valley is a simple delight.
Enormous steep cliffs made of granite abound,
Covered in plants nowhere else to be found.
If hiking and camping is your cup of tea,
Yosemite Park is the right place to be.

# FLORIDA KEYS

If tropical weather makes your heart warm,
Visit miles of islands that call Florida home.
Swim in crystal clear water, enjoy, and have fun,
While spending your days in the beautiful sun.

With abundance of coral and fish on display,
Seeing life underwater will take your breath away.
Listen to birds and strange animal sounds,
And discover bright flowers that grow all around.
Whatever your plans are, you will want to return,
To the islands with so much to see and to learn.

Thank you for joining our explorations.
We saw cool and exciting US destinations.

This story is ending, but we all can assume,
Another Arthur adventure will be coming soon!

Thank you for reading. If you enjoyed this book, please consider leaving an honest review at your favorite store.

Check out more books about Arthur in the Kids Books For Young Explorers series

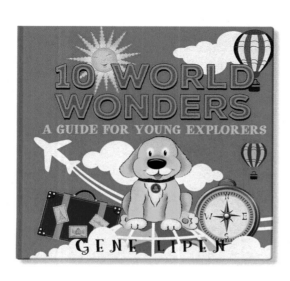

# FUN COLORING PAGES

Enjoy!

I LIKE THIS BOOK, BECAUSE:

_____

_____

Made in the USA
Monee, IL
07 December 2022

20136449R00019